The Short Book on Options

A Conservative Strategy for the Buy and Hold Investor

By

Mark D. Wolfinger

D1051194

ISBN: 1-4033-0775-X (e-book)
ISBN: 1-4033-0776-8 (Paperback)

Disclaimer

The information presented in this book is for educational purposes only. I neither make nor suggest any specific recommendations for investment. Examples are for illustrative purposes only, and serve to show what may happen in a particular situation. The possible rewards are stated, as are the possible risks. Covered call writing is a sound, conservative investment strategy, but losses can still occur.

This book is printed on acid free paper.

1stBooks - rev. 06/06/02

This book is gratefully dedicated to my life partner

Penny Rotheiser

Acknowledgments

I thank those friends who made useful contributions to this project. They gave their time and energy: Ric Birch, Elisa Castellon, Camden McKinley, Wes Shriver, Cheryl Jefferson, Irv Kessler, and James Rohan.

An extra special thank you to those who made major contributions: Carol Haag, who gave much of her time, and whose advice was right on the money; June Shriver, Frank Belyan, and Penny Rotheiser, who read every word and not only gave very useful advice that changed the content of the book, but who also carefully edited the final product.

Thank you all.

Table of Contents

x

Foreword

The majority of the investing public, and I assume you are in that group, are unaware of the possible benefits you can gain from the conservative use of stock options. Many are not aware that stock options exist. By the time you finish reading this book you will know how to use options to:

- Increase the probability of making a profit on your stock holdings

- Provide your portfolio with some protection, if your stocks go down

In easy to understand language, you learn a low risk strategy for the options markets. You learn to consistently achieve a rate of return on your investments that is probably much better than you earn without the use of options. This strategy makes your overall portfolio safer by providing some insurance against loss. This is a real benefit in years when the market declines. The investment strategy is based on adopting a simple technique using call options. (If you are not sure what call options are, options basics are explained in Chapter 2.)

This book is for you, if you are a buy and hold investor. You learn how to gain an advantage over your current methods. Those investors who use options have an edge over those who don't.

This book is for you, if you are an investor who does your own research and decides for yourself which stocks to buy.

This book is for you, if you are a member of an investment club. As investors interested in growth and who carefully research which stocks to own, investment club members are in a position to benefit from the use of call options.

This book is for you, if you have a self-directed retirement account. The investment technique taught in these pages is the only options strategy investors are permitted to use in retirement accounts, as it is the only strategy considered sufficiently conservative for such accounts. It is especially useful for these accounts, where earnings are allowed to compound year after year. If you take advantage of the strategy outlined in this volume, those extra earnings make your financially secure retirement more likely.

Because options have received bad press over the years, many people close their ears when they hear the word 'options'. I approached the president of an investment club and offered to present a complimentary talk about the advantages of using options to her club. Her reply was "We don't do that." I felt badly because her lack of curiosity deprived other club members of their opportunity to learn about options. They were unable to decide if they want to use options for either their own investment accounts or for the club account.

A friend spoke to a professional investment advisor about the possibility of using the basic options strategy I describe in these pages as another investment tool that he could share with his clients. The investment advisor had no interest in learning about the subject.

Apathy. Lack of information. Bad publicity. I faced all of them when I tried to build a business based on teaching my favorite investment tool to others. These three factors became the driving force that inspired me to write this short volume. My goal is to produce a short, instructive book on the subject. I hope the word spreads, and that conservative option strategies find their rightful place in the investment world.

Evanston, Illinois. February, 2002

Introduction

This book presents a simple technique for using stock options that you can apply to your own stock portfolio. Under most market conditions, if you adopt this strategy, you can produce substantial additional income. This trading tool is not some closely guarded secret, although it might as well be, since most investors do not know this easily understood strategy is available. Some professional investment advisors, who could have been teaching this investment tool to their clients over the past (almost) three decades, have failed to do so. One purpose of this book is to clear away misconceptions and fears about options and to make information readily available so that investors can decide if they want to take advantage of stock options.

Negative publicity has hounded options trading since the market in tulip options collapsed in the 17th century. At that time, speculators, who chose a very risky strategy using put options, (if you are not sure what put options are, options basics are explained in Chapter 2) defaulted and were unable to fulfill their obligations when tulip prices fell sharply.

Quite often, the media reports on the negative side of business because it is newsworthy. Options have received negative coverage over the years, for there is no news to report when people use options intelligently to reduce risk and increase profits. When speculators cause disasters, such as the collapse of the Barings Bank in 1995, the press is there to cover the story.[1]

Today, many people turn away from options and decline, when offered the opportunity to learn how to use them. Thus, investors are not aware of the benefits to be gained from using stock options. The truth is, options can be used conservatively to produce additional earnings, but many people mistakenly believe only speculators use options. Despite the fact that additional profits are the most likely result when using options in the suggested manner, as with other sound investment techniques, losses can still occur.

There are some people who make a living by promoting options as a get-rich-quick mechanism. There are others who make outrageous claims about potential profits and charge exorbitant fees for seminars. I make no such claims. I am only telling you that by using options there is a high probability your investment account will be more profitable than a similar account that does not use options. In order to gain this additional income, you must give up something. This book includes a discussion of what you have to sacrifice in order to obtain the benefits of using options. This very conservative option strategy has some risk, and that risk is discussed in this book.

The strategy that I teach in this volume is not for everyone, but if you invest in individual stocks, this

---

[1] The venerable British Barings Bank collapsed in February 1995 after a rogue futures trader lost huge sums.

book will be an eye-opener for you. If you give up the small chance to make a bonanza on any of your stock positions, you gain a high probability chance to earn a significant additional profit on those stocks.

One of the tried and true methods for accumulating wealth is to take profits from investments and, instead of spending them, allow them to be reinvested. This is called compounding. When you become educated in the world of stock options, when you are able to utilize the simple strategy outlined in these pages to generate additional income year after year, and if you have the ability to allow your earnings to compound over time, you will find you are building wealth more rapidly than you ever thought possible.[2] Retirement accounts are the perfect vehicles for this compounding strategy, for they have the added benefit of having all taxes deferred until you take the money. That allows you even greater compounding capabilities, since the government's share of your profits is allowed to remain in the account and grow. By all means, consider using what you learn from this book to strengthen your IRA or other retirement accounts.

There are many investors who buy stocks and never sell them. You will learn how the buy and hold investment strategy can be improved by adopting the methods taught in these pages. It is prudent for you, as a buy and hold investor, to periodically review your investments, because the stock you bought some time ago is not necessarily a good investment today. If you

---

[2] See Appendix B, Table B.1 for data on compounding.

learn to apply the strategy described in this book to your current stock positions, some of your stagnant positions will begin to earn additional income, and you can use options to get higher (than current market) prices for any stocks you decide to sell

Options will play a significant role in your investment future, but <u>the overall performance of your portfolio will depend primarily on the performance of your stocks</u>.

If you have questions as you progress through the book, ask me:

Send email to: mark@mdwoptions.com

If you are ready to learn about options, let's begin with a brief history of options trading.

Chapter 1

Recent Options Trading History

The Chicago Board Options Exchange (CBOE) began trading equity options in April 1973, and revolutionized the way those options were traded. With the listing of options on an exchange, the contracts became standardized with specific and predictable expiration dates and strike prices.[3]   (If these terms are unfamiliar to you, options basics are explained in the next chapter.)   A marketplace was established, so that a customer was able to sell an option that he had bought earlier, or buy an option that he had previously sold.

Before options were traded on an exchange, trading in puts and calls had been complicated.   Brokers and dealers advertised specific options for sale in the Wall Street Journal.   These option contracts had random exercise dates and strike prices. If you bought one of those options, there was little chance you would be able to sell it to anyone before expiration. The advent of exchange-listed options at the CBOE changed all that.

The CBOE began by listing options in 16 stocks.   As the popularity of these options grew, as trading volume

---

[3] Standardized: strike prices are set at specific intervals for all stocks. Strikes are available every 2½ points for strike prices 5 through 25; every 5 points through 200; then every 10 points thereafter.

expanded, three other exchanges (American Stock Exchange, Philadelphia Stock Exchange, Pacific Coast Stock Exchange) began trading options in the mid 1970's. Today options on over 2000 stocks and many indexes are listed on one or more of these four options exchanges.

Individuals, hedge funds, and institutional investors have used options. Options play a significant role in the investment world, and are one of the most useful investment tools available today. Yet, they are unknown to the majority of investors. Some professionals spread the word that options are speculative tools and are not suitable for use by the ordinary investor. Nothing could be further from the truth. What *is* true is when the market collapsed in October 1987, too many people owned speculative and dangerous positions using put options. When the market suffered a huge loss on that one dismal day in October, speculators lost far more than they thought possible

When the smoke cleared, when the fortunes were lost, some professionals made statements to the effect that options were substantially to blame for the debacle. They made the decision to steer customers away from options trading, much to the detriment of those customers. One major brokerage house established such stringent requirements for opening an options account, they virtually prevented their customers from trading options. The employees working for that brokerage house were instructed not to trade options, and to discourage their customers from trading options.

It has been this way for years. The professionals fail to educate their customers about the major benefits of options trading. They do not tell their customers about the very conservative ways in which options can be used. Thus, many people today do not have information regarding options that would benefit them.

This book was written to help the average investor learn to use the options markets in a conservative, intelligent manner. In addition to providing additional income, options can be used to reduce your exposure to the vagaries of the marketplace. Imagine: options can be used to reduce the risk of your stock portfolio!

Chapter 2

Options Basics

Because this book is intended to show the average investor he can profitably use the options markets, we must begin at the beginning. That requires an explanation of what an option is and how an option works - both in our everyday lives and in the stock market.

Optionspeak

Some of the terms used in the options world will be new to you. The first time these terms appear in the text, they are indicated in bold. The more important terms are also underlined. Definitions are in the glossary (Appendix A). Don't worry, there aren't too many of them.

What is an option?

An **option** is a contract between two parties: the buyer of the option and the seller of the option. The price the option buyer pays is called the **premium**.

There are two types of options:

A **call** option gives its owner the right to buy.

A **put** option gives its owner the right to sell.

In return for the payment of the option premium, the call owner has the right to buy (and the put owner has the right to sell):

- A specified item (called the **underlying** asset)

- At a specified price (called the **strike** price)

- For a specified period of time (from now until the **expiration** date)

Thus:

A *call* option gives its owner the right (but not the obligation) to *buy* the underlying at the strike price at any time from now until the expiration date.

A *put* option gives its owner the right (but not the obligation) to *sell* the underlying at the strike price at any time from now until the expiration date.

That is all there is to an option. It really is a simple concept.

How does an option work?

The option gives its buyer certain **rights** and imparts certain **obligations** on the seller.

If the option owner elects to do what the contract allows, and if he does it before the expiration date, then he is said to **exercise** his rights. He now either buys (if it is a call option) or sells (if it is a put option) the underlying asset at the strike price. The option seller is **assigned** an exercise notice and is obligated to fulfill the conditions of the contract by either selling (to the call exerciser) or buying (from the put exerciser) the underlying asset at the strike price.

Again, that's all there is to it.

In order to give you a clearer understanding of the process, here are some examples of options at work in our every day world.

Options in our daily lives

You may not be aware, but you have probably seen and used options many times. At the supermarket, have you ever found the store was out of a product on special sale? When that happened the customer service department gave you a rain check for that item. That rain check is a call option, because it gives you the right to purchase the sale item (underlying) at the sale price (strike price) for a definite period of time (until expiration). You have no obligation to make that purchase, but have the right to do so. Since the rain check was free, the premium is zero. If you later (before the rain check expires) return to the store to exercise your option, then the store manager is assigned[4] and is obligated to deliver to you the underlying at the strike price.

---

[4] When the customer hands the rain check to the store manager (or cashier) and tells him that he wants to exercise his rights, that is the assignment notice.

If you take public transportation and buy a transfer, that transfer is a call option on a second ride. In Chicago, a transfer expires two hours after it is issued. If you sometimes finish your business in less than two hours, and use public transportation to go to and from that business, then it is probably a good investment to risk 30 cents to buy a transfer. The transfer gives you the right, but not the obligation, to take that second ride (underlying) within the two hours (expiration) for no additional charge (strike price is zero). If you are not ready to return home within that time period, then you will not use the transfer and allow it to expire. In that case, you will have lost your total investment of 30 cents. However, if you finish your business within the allotted time and exercise your option by giving the transfer to the bus driver,[5] then you will not have to pay an additional fare of $1.50. Under these conditions, the option proves to be a very sound investment.

These are only two examples of options that we take for granted. In the next chapter we take an in depth look at the various choices available when you use these common options. It is my hope that the day will come when the use of stock options will be commonplace.

---

[5] This is the driver's notification that he has been assigned an exercise notice, and he is obligated to deliver the free ride to the transfer owner.

Chapter 3

The *Options* When Using An Option

This chapter is devoted to understanding what you can do with a call option. As an example, we use a situation in which you have a written agreement allowing you to buy an item at a sale price for a limited time. We examine various scenarios and learn a few additional optionspeak terms. Once you gain a thorough understanding of how this option works, you will know how a stock option works, for they are essentially identical. There are differences, but those differences do not come into play when you consider your choices when using call options.

Assume that you are a dog enthusiast. You want to buy a purebred golden retriever puppy that you plan to train to be a show dog. You notice a breeder in a nearby town is having a 2-day sale on the puppies that interest you. You are unable to get there for the first day, but arrive on the afternoon of the second sale date. You find that it has been a very successful sale and all the puppies have new homes. You express your disappointment to the breeder who tells you that he has another litter of similar retriever puppies, but they are currently too young to leave his farm. He tells you to return in 3 or 4 weeks when he will have a few more available. He explains that the puppies will be old enough to sell by that time, and if do you return, he will honor the sale price for you.

He gives you a signed letter granting the bearer the right to purchase a golden retriever puppy from the specific litter that he described to you for the current sale price, which is $200 less than his usual price. The special deal is available for only 4 weeks. You happily accept the letter and go home. You are the owner of a call option, because you have the right to purchase the puppy (underlying) for the sale price (strike price) as long as you do it within 4 weeks (expiration date). You paid a premium of zero for this call option.

Now let's look at the various actions available to you when using your call option:

Option One

When you return to the breeder's farm, it is almost 4 weeks later. He remembers you and shows you three puppies from which you can choose. One puppy comes right up and licks your face, so the choice has been made. You give him the letter and pay the sale price, and he delivers the puppy to you. Without the letter, the puppy would have cost $200 more.

- What happened?

    o You exercised your rights as the option owner and bought the underlying at the strike price before the expiration.

    o The breeder was assigned an exercise notice and sold the underlying at the strike price.

Note that the market price of the puppy was higher than the strike price. When this happens, the option is said to be **in-the-money** or it has **intrinsic value**. The intrinsic value is the difference between the market price and the strike price ($200 in this example) and is the amount you saved by exercising the option.

Option Two

You are having second thoughts. You still love the idea of a new puppy, but are not sure if you want to cope with the time and expense necessary to train a dog to be a show animal. You pay a return visit to the breeder's farm two weeks later to take another look. You know the puppies are too young to leave the farm, but if you see them again it may help you make up your mind.

As you are admiring the puppies and trying to decide what to do, you strike up a conversation with a couple who is also looking at the puppies. They tell you they plan to return in two weeks to purchase one of these puppies. They are not aware they missed a sale, but are anxiously waiting until one of the pups is old enough to come home with them. You both agree the price is steep, but they are willing to pay it. Since you are uncertain about getting a dog, you decide that if you can make a profit you are willing to forego the pleasure of taking one of these puppies home. You explain to the couple that you have a letter from the breeder granting the bearer the right to buy one of the puppies for a $200 discount. You tell them that you are uncertain about whether to purchase a puppy, but you are willing to split that $200 savings with them. You offer to sell the letter (if you call it a call option, you will confuse this couple) for $100. They agree.

- What happened?

  o You sold your option and have a profit of $100. You no longer have any right to buy the puppy for the sale price.

  o The couple has invested $100. They plan to return in two weeks to exercise the option. If they do, they will save $100 (They can purchase the puppy for a discount of $200, but paid you $100). If they do not use the letter, they will lose their $100 investment.

Option Three

When you return to the breeder's farm the day before the option expires, you find the place is in disarray. There are large moving trucks and many people are running around shouting orders. You eventually learn there has been a tragedy. Although you do not know the details, the bottom line is that the breeder is moving out of town immediately and is selling everything he can. There are two puppies from the specified litter available, and they are for sale. The price is an additional $200 less than the original sale price. The breeder assures you that his personal problems have nothing to do with the dogs, and they are in excellent health, so you buy one. You are sorry for the breeder's misfortune, but it turns out to be a bargain for you. There is no need to show the option (letter) to the breeder, for you have no intention of using it. You have the right, but not the obligation, to pay the strike price. Instead you ignore the option and pay $200 less than you expected to pay.

- What happened?

    o You have purchased the underlying for less than the strike price. When this happens, the option is said to be **out-of-the-money**.

    o Your option is going to **expire worthless**, because you are not going to exercise it.

Summary. There are three things that you can do with a call option.

- Exercise it

- Sell it

- Allow it to expire worthless

These are the identical things you can do with a stock option, for they work in exactly the same way.

By now you should feel comfortable with the language of options and confident that you understand how options work. We are going to move away from familiar options, and enter the world of stock options.

Chapter 4

Stock Options

The underlying asset of a stock option is stock (almost always 100 shares). Options are traded on one of the four options exchanges (listed below). These options are described in the following format:

> IBM Apr 110 call   or   MSFT Jan 65 put

The former option represents the right to buy (call) 100 shares of IBM stock (underlying) for $110 (strike price) per share at any time between now and the expiration of the option next April.

The latter option represents the right to sell (put) 100 shares of Microsoft for $65 per share at any time before expiration next January.

The last day of trading for stock options is the <u>third Friday of the expiration month</u>. The technical expiration date is the next day, Saturday, but if you want to exercise an option, the cutoff time is Friday afternoon, shortly after the market closes.

If an option owner wants to exercise his rights to either buy (if it is a call option) or sell (if it is a put option) the underlying stock at the strike price, he calls and instructs his broker to exercise the option(s). The broker then notifies the **Options Clearing Corporation (OCC)** of the exercise. The OCC is a clearinghouse for information about who owns, and who has sold, every outstanding options contract. The OCC verifies you own this option and have the right to exercise it. Next it selects, at random, one of the accounts that had previously sold the identical option. That account owner is assigned an **exercise notice**, and must fulfill the conditions of the contract by either selling or buying the underlying asset at the strike price.

Trading call or put options

Today, stock options are traded on four exchanges:

AMEX   The American Stock Exchange in N.Y.
CBOE   The Chicago Board Options Exchange
PHLX   The Philadelphia Stock Exchange
PCST   The Pacific Coast Stock Exchange in S. F.

The Options Clearing Corporation (OCC) was founded in 1973 and is the issuer and registered clearing facility for all U.S. exchange listed equity options. In English, this means that the OCC keeps records for all outstanding contracts. It knows who is **long** (owns) and who is **short** (has sold, without owning) every outstanding options contract.

For readers with Internet access, the addresses of these exchanges and the OCC are:

AMEX: http://www.amex.com/
CBOE: http://www.cboe.com/
PHLX: http://www.phlx.com/index.stm

PCST: http://www.pacificex.com/
OCC: http://www.optionsclearing.com

Placing an option order is exactly the same as placing a stock order. If you use a live broker, you simply call and tell the broker which option you want to buy or sell. You also tell the broker how many contracts, and state a price (for a limit order) or say that you want to place a market order, if you are willing to accept the best available price at the time the order arrives on the trading floor. Most brokers require that you have the necessary funds (either to pay for the option or to cover any **margin** requirements) in your account before they accept the order.

If you already have an open brokerage account, you can place a stock order with your broker. However, this is not the case with stock options. Even though option orders are entered in the same way as stock orders, there are a few necessary steps to take before any broker accepts your first option order.

Getting started trading options

Your broker will require you to open a **margin account**. You will not have to trade on margin, i.e., you will not be required to borrow money from your broker in order to trade options, but you will be required to have a margin account. Think of having a margin account as owning another call option. You have the right, but not the obligation, to borrow money from your broker, if you ever so desire.

In order to sell options against your long stock positions (the term **write** is often used to describe the selling of a call option when you own the stock), you must deposit the stock certificates with your broker. Today few investors keep their stock certificates, but if you are one of them, you will not be able to participate in the strategies outlined in this book.

Before you make your first option trade, the broker is required to send you copies of **Characteristics and Risks of Standardized Options** and **Understanding Stock Options**, two educational pamphlets. These publications contain useful information for the options novice. Copies are available online:

http://www.
optionsclearing.com/publications/risks/riskchap1.jsp

or

http://www.
optionsclearing.com/publications/uso/usointro.jsp

Additional information about getting started with options can be found at:

http://www.mdwoptions.com/Getstarted.htm

Once you have read your pamphlets and opened a margin account, you can place an option order with your broker. Thus, the question is: Why would you want to place an option order? That is the topic of the next chapter, and the main focus of this book.

Chapter 5

Why Enter An Option Order?

Options are versatile instruments and there are a variety of strategies you can adopt when using them. Some are conservative, some are highly speculative, and some fall between the extremes. It is beyond the scope of this book to teach you how to become an options specialist or to prepare you for a career as an options trader. The intent is to demonstrate how one conservative options strategy can be used to help you increase the earnings from your stock portfolio, and to teach you that strategy. The rationale is: <u>if being conservative can make you substantial extra income, why would you want to consider speculative approaches?</u>

The strategy is called **covered call writing**. This means that for every 100 shares of stock you own, you will consider selling one call option. In other words, you are going to sell to someone else the right to purchase your stock at a price you choose. You are also going to select from among four expiration dates. Each stock position requires a decision. The first decision is whether you are going to sell a call option, or simply hold the stock.

We are only going to discuss selling a call option when you own the stock. Although it is possible to sell call options when you do not own the stock (**uncovered**

call), this type of trade is so risky,[6] we are not going to mention it again in this book. In fact, most brokerage houses do not allow you to make that type of trade, and those that do require a large deposit of margin money to protect them against loss. When we sell a call, it is only when the call is covered - i.e., when you own the stock so you can deliver it, in the event you are assigned an exercise notice.

The obvious questions are

- Why would you want to sell a call option?

- What do you have to gain?

- What do you have to lose?

- Can this simple strategy really make a significant difference in the value of your portfolio?

Let's review what happens if you sell a call option. In return for paying a premium to you, the buyer of the call option obtains the right to purchase 100 shares of your specific stock at the strike price for a specified period of time. In return for receiving the premium, you have the obligation to sell 100 shares of the

---

[6] If you sell a call option and the stock rises higher than the strike price, you will be assigned at expiration. You will be forced to go to the market and buy the stock so you can deliver it. Since there is, in theory, no limit to how high the stock can go, the loss is potentially unlimited.

specified stock at the strike price - but only if the owner of the call option exercises his rights before the option expires. As the seller of the call, you have no part in the decision as to if or when you sell the stock. That decision rests with the owner of the call option.

Why would you want to sell a call option? What do you have to gain?

Our discussion is easier to follow if we use an example. Let's assume you own 200 shares of a stock that you have held for some time. You still want to own the stock. Yet, if the stock were to trade at a higher price you would be glad to sell it. That is the perfect scenario for a covered call writing program. Another situation in which you would want to consider using this strategy occurs when you own a stock that has not been making any money for you. You want to generate income from this stock, and you are reluctant to sell it at the current price.

Assume the stock symbol is XYZ, the stock is trading for 38 and you are willing to sell it for 40 per share. You can place a good 'til cancelled (GTC) order with your broker to sell the stock if it reaches your price of 40. If you do that, there is nothing else to do, except to wait and remember you have that order outstanding. If the stock is sold, your broker will notify you of the sale. If the stock does not trade as high as your price, then you will not sell it

As an alternative to placing the sell order, you can sell someone else the right to buy your stock for 40. If you do, you receive a cash premium immediately, and it is yours to keep (the premium is not a down payment; it is a payment for the option), regardless of whether or not the call buyer eventually buys your stock for 40. For this example, we sell a call option with about six months remaining until expiration. In practice, there are four expirations available for each stock. They range from the current month to either 6 or 7 or 8 months in the future. No stock offers expirations in all months, but there is always a choice of four expirations. There are some options (called **LEAPS**) with much longer expirations, and there is a short discussion about them in chapter 14. We are not going to sell LEAPS.

As you will see in Chapter 8, the premium you can expect to receive varies over a wide range and is dependent on several factors. We make the following assumptions:

- You sell an option with approximately six months until expiration

- The strike price of the option is near the stock price. In our example, the stock is 38 and the strike is 40

- You receive a premium of 10 to 25% of the stock price for each call. In our example, the premium is $400 per option

Example

- You own 200 XYZ; market price 38
- You sell 2 XYZ 40-strike calls with six months to expiration. The price is 4

Note: Just as 100 shares of a stock priced at 38 is worth $3800, an option priced at 4 means the option is $4 per share, so one contract, which can be exercised for 100 shares of stock, is $400.

What happens now?

1) You receive the proceeds from the option sale, or $800, less commissions. (Commissions vary, so ask your broker what he charges). The cash goes into your account the next business day and starts to earn interest.

2) You continue to own the XYZ stock, but will not be able to sell it unless you buy back the calls. (Reason: If you sell the stock, your position would consist of an uncovered call, and your broker will not let you hold such dangerous positions. Even if the broker allows it, you should not want to do so, for it is not consistent with our conservative strategy.) If the stock pays a dividend, you will receive it.[7]

3) That's it.

---

[7] Later in this chapter is a discussion of the risk of not receiving the dividend.

What happens next?

On occasion, you are assigned an exercise notice before expiration and you sell your stock for the strike price. This early exercise is most likely to occur if the stock pays a dividend and the option owner decides to exercise the option early in order to collect that dividend. Otherwise, early exercise does not happen often enough for us to consider it further, so we assume time has passed and it is now after the market has closed on expiration day.

Scenario one

XYZ stock is below the strike price of 40, and the option is out-of-the-money. Whoever owns the option will not want to buy your stock for 40. If that person wants the stock, he can go to the marketplace and buy it for less. The main point for you is that the option is going to expire worthless. You are no longer under any obligation to sell your stock for 40, or for any other price. You keep the premium ($800) you received. Next Monday morning, when the market opens, or any time thereafter, you can sell another two options against your 200 shares of stock. If you were to sell a new option before the current option has officially expired, it would be an uncovered sale. That is too dangerous for our conservative strategy.

This is a satisfactory result. You are better off by the entire proceeds ($800) from the option sale than you would have been if you had stayed with your previous strategy of holding the stock and doing nothing.

Scenario two

XYZ stock closed at 40, and the option is **at-the-money**. You do not know whether or not the person who owns the call options will take your stock. You must wait until next Monday morning. You then call your broker (or check your account online) to find out whether or not you have been assigned on your call options. Some brokers are inefficient when it comes to letting you know, so be certain to call before the market opens. If you have not been assigned, you are free to write calls against that stock again. If you have been assigned, you no longer have a position in this stock, but have the proceeds from the sale. You must decide how, or if, you are going to reinvest that money.

This is a satisfactory result. You have the proceeds from the sale of the options. In addition, your stock has increased in value by $2 per share. If you are assigned, that is a good result, since you both sold the stock for the price that you wanted and you have the money from the sale of the calls. If you did not sell your stock, that is also a good result because you can now sell the stock, or sell options again and collect another premium.

Scenario three

XYZ finishes above 40. You are assigned and must sell your stock for the strike price. You no longer have a position in XYZ stock.

This is a satisfactory result for you. Not only do you keep the premium received from the sale of the options, you also sold the stock for your price.

The above discussion illustrates why you would consider selling a call option. You make more money compared with simply buying the stock and holding it under a variety of market conditions.

If all of the possible results are satisfactory, why doesn't everyone do this? What can go wrong? What are the risks? These are good questions, and the answers are considered next.

What do you have to lose? What can go wrong?

Although covered call writing is a conservative strategy, there is some risk associated with it:

1) If your stock makes a major move down, you will have a loss. The premium you receive from the call sale may not be sufficient to cover the entire loss.

   If you are a buy and hold investor and therefore would not sell the stock during the decline, then this is not a risk factor for you. In fact you will be glad you sold the option, for it reduces your loss.

   If you change your mind and sell the stock during such a decline in price, it is necessary to buy back the option you previously sold. You will have a profit on the sale of the call, but you must buy it back in order to sell your stock. If you sell the stock without buying the option, you are left with an uncovered call position, and that is too risky.

2) If your main objective was to sell the stock (40 in our example), you might lose the sale. For example, if the stock price climbs above 40 during the life of the option, and falls below that price at expiration, the call owner will not exercise his option and you will not sell your stock. If you entered a good 'til cancelled sell order, the stock would have automatically been sold when it reached your price. If the price decline (after it trades at 40) is sufficiently large, you will be unhappy with the current price of the stock. The gain from the sale of the call reduces the loss, but you still own the stock.

3) If your stock rises through the strike price and makes a major advance, you will have lost the opportunity to sell the stock at the higher price because you sold the call option. You still have a good profit (some mistakenly believe they lost money in this situation), but this profit is less than you could have made without the option sale. However, if you had entered a good 'til cancelled sell order, you would have sold the stock before the large price increase.

4) If you own a dividend paying stock, it is possible you will not collect the dividend. The owner of the call option has the right to exercise the call at any time. It is possible he will choose the day before

the stock goes ex-dividend. That means you will be assigned and must sell your stock and not receive the dividend. This is not all bad news, since you sell the stock at the price (strike price) you wanted. In addition, this sale occurs before expiration, and you are able to reinvest the proceeds of the sale and put the money back to work.

There is another risk associated with selling call options. It is impossible to quantify, for it is a psychological risk. Some people want the best of all possible worlds every time, and are never satisfied with less. This topic is discussed in more detail in Chapter 13.

Those are the major risks associated with selling covered calls. I believe these risks are small when compared with the benefits available from using call options, and that most investors should at least consider using options in this manner.

When you compare the buy and hold strategy with the covered call strategy:

- Selling the call allows you to you make **more** (or lose less) money if your stock goes down

- Selling the call allows you to you make **more** money if your stock is unchanged

- Selling the call allows you to make **more** money if your stock goes up a small amount

- Selling the call makes you **less** money if your stock goes up a sufficiently large amount. You still do well; you still make good money, but not as much as you could have made

There is a saying on Wall Street: "Sometimes the bulls win, sometimes the bears win, but the pigs always lose." Don't be greedy. Invest wisely, take good profits, take them often, and allow the earnings to compound over time. You will do very well by making good returns on many trades, even if occasionally you miss out on a bonanza.

Does this strategy really make a difference?

Yes. It does. Most of the time, when expiration rolls around (sometimes it will seem like forever before it arrives), you will be pleased you sold the option. Once in awhile, you would have done better without the call sale. Over the long run, there will be many more profitable outcomes, and you will probably have more money in your investment account if you adopt the covered call writing strategy.

Let's begin to take a more detailed look at the numbers in the next chapter. That will make it easier for you to compare strategies.

Chapter 6

Let's Take A Look At The Arithmetic

We'll continue with the example from the previous chapter. You own a stock, currently priced at 38. You sell a 6-month call option with a strike price of 40, and collect a premium of 4. How much money do you have invested in this position?

You can sell your stock for $3800, so you have to consider you have that amount invested in the stock. Because you received $400 cash from the call sale, your investment has been reduced by that amount.

Original Investment	$3800
Less: Option Premium	-$ 400
Net Investment	$3400

Thus, you have a current investment of $3400 in the covered call position. If you hold this position, and do nothing until the option expires, there are two possibilities:

Expiration possibilities

    A. If the stock is over 40 at expiration, you will be assigned on the call option. You must sell your stock and your position becomes $4000 in cash (less a commission on the stock sale). This represents a net profit of $600 on a $3400 investment, or a return of 17.65%.

Sell stock at strike price.	$4000
Less Net Investment	- $3400
Profit (Before Commissions)	$ 600

Return = Profit ÷ Net Investment
= 600 ÷ 3400 = 17.65%

This is a very good return. If you continue to earn money at that pace, and compound those earnings, it takes just over two years to double your money. It is not difficult to see how quickly returns like these, if continued for a number of years, can lead to accumulated wealth. (See Appendix B for sample compounding calculations.)

B. If the stock remains below the strike price and the call expires worthless, you are better off by $400 (for each option you sold). You will not have made the maximum possible profit, but you have $400 per option you would not have otherwise. You can consider you received a dividend of $400 on your $3400 investment over a 6-month period. That is a return of 11.76%. This is 11.76% more than you would have made if you held the stock and did not sell the call.

Return = Profit ÷ Investment = 400 ÷ 3400 = 11.76%

If you are assigned on the call, you earn the maximum possible from your position. That is an excellent result, as it is the best you can do. Even so, the less experienced investor gets confused and feels that something bad happened if the option does not expire worthless. If worthless, he can see that the entire option premium has become income - income he would not have without the sale of the call. If the option is in-the-money, the less experienced investor often feels he made less money that he should have, for he has to sell his stock below the current market price. *Don't fall into that trap.* If you are assigned, you make the maximum available to you. Once the decision to sell the call has been made, there is a maximum potential profit, so be glad when you make that amount.

You made your profit, but what did it cost you?

What did you give up in order to collect this additional "dividend" on your stock? You gave up the *potential* for a much larger gain. But look at what you gained - insurance in the event the stock declined in price, and you increased the chances that your position would be profitable at expiration.

Did you really increase the chance that the position would be profitable? Yes you did. It is more likely to be profitable, because the stock has a better chance to finish above 34 (your reduced cost) than it does to finish above 38 (the cost without the option sale). If you are not sure why it is more likely to be over 34 than it is to be over 38, see footnote 20.

It is difficult to place a dollar value on the protection you received. Insurance is not free, and it is worth something to know you will not lose money if your stock declines in value by a certain amount (4 points in our example). It is also difficult to place a value on the increased probability that your position will be profitable at expiration - but it does have value. To me, the combination of protection and a more likely profit is better than the hope the stock goes up in price.

Every investor should look at the risks and rewards to determine if this strategy is suitable for him. I believe a careful consideration of the details leads many people to believe adopting this strategy is the right thing to do - even if it is only for part of their portfolio. For me, it is an easy decision. I want those solid, steady returns again and again. It is a winning strategy to make extra money many times, and only occasionally settle for less.

The additional profit available from writing call options represents a significant percentage increase in the return on your investments. Think about this - what would you say to someone who told you he knew how to safely increase your annual portfolio profits by even 5% per year. Wouldn't you want to learn about it so you could consider it? Selling those call options allows you to make substantial extra income. In the example cited above, the additional annualized return was over 23% (11.76% for six months), even without an increase in the price of the stock. As you will see in Chapters 9 and 10, the amount of potential income is dependent on the type of stocks you own and on how conservative you are in choosing which option to sell. Remember, you are investing in the stock market, so your results will primarily be determined by the performance of the stocks in your portfolio. Options can be used to enhance that performance.

Because there is a choice of options to sell, and because not everyone makes the same choice, there are different results for different investors. Some take a more aggressive approach, taking more risk and aiming for a greater profit. Others seek capital gains in addition to the option premium. Some are more concerned with safety than with capital gains. There is something in the covered call writing approach that is suitable for your goals and temperament. It is fun to determine which strategy, or mix of strategies, is best for you. Remember the reason for using a call writing strategy is that it is a conservative investment tool. Minimizing risk should be a constant concern. In Chapter 10 we take a closer look at which option choices are more aggressive and which are more conservative.

Chapter 7

How Options Are Priced

When you want to buy or sell an option, you will find a market for that option, i.e., there are traders (called **market makers** or specialists) who continuously post both <u>bid</u> prices (what they are willing to pay from sellers) and <u>offer</u> prices (what they are asking buyers to pay) for that option. The option you want to trade may be listed on only one, or up to all four of the options exchanges. The more exchanges listing the specific options that interest you, the tighter[8] the markets are likely to be (although this is not always the case). Professional traders do not choose random numbers for their bids and offers. They use a complex mathematical formula to calculate a theoretical value for each option, which helps them determine their bid and offer prices.

The traders do not strictly adhere to the formula when making buy and sell decisions. They use the theoretical value as a starting point for determining the prices of options in the marketplace. Market conditions, such as supply and demand, influence option prices.

---

[8] Tighter market means the difference between the bid price and the ask price is smaller. This is favorable for the customer.

Theoretical value

We will not delve into details of the mathematics, but the following factors are used in the formula that determines an option's theoretical value:

- **Stock price**

  o The higher the price of the stock, the more a specific call option is worth and the less a specific put option is worth. The right to buy a stock for 50 is worth more if the stock is 50 than if it is 48.

- **Strike Price**

  o The higher the strike price, the less a call is worth. This is intuitive, since the right to buy at 45 per share must be worth less than the right to buy at 40 per share.

  o The higher the strike price, the more a put is worth. The right to sell at 45 is worth more than the right to sell at 40.

- **Volatility**

  o Options are worth more as stock volatility increases. The option buyer hopes the stock makes a big move in the correct direction. Since a volatile stock makes big moves much more often than a non-volatile stock, option buyers pay much more when the underlying is volatile. This is a <u>major</u> factor in determining the price of the option in the marketplace. A detailed discussion of volatility can be found in Chapter 9.

o   Long-term options are affected more than short-term options when volatilities are changed.

- **Time remaining** until expiration

  o   The more time, the more the option is worth. More time gives the underlying stock a greater opportunity to make a move favorable to the option owner (who can then sell his option for his profit). The buyer is willing to pay for that increased chance.

- **Interest rate**

  o   This is a less important factor, but the higher the interest rate, the more a call is worth. An investor buys a call option instead of buying stock. Since the option costs less than the stock, buying the option gives the investor extra cash on which he can earn interest. The more interest earned, the more the buyer is willing to pay for the call option.

o The higher the interest rate, the less a put option is worth.

- **Dividend**

  o On the day when a stock first trades ex-dividend (without the dividend), the stock price drops by the amount of that dividend. Since this results in a lower stock price, the larger the dividend, the less a call (and the more a put) is worth.

Summary: There are several factors that go into the formula used to calculate the theoretical value of an option. The major factors are volatility, stock price, strike price, and time. The minor factors are interest rate and dividend.

By being aware of these factors, you will understand why the premium of an option changes.

Chapter 8

The Numbers

For easy reference, this chapter is devoted to data. It contains the numbers discussed in chapters 9 and 10. Data is presented in seven tables. It will be easier for you to study the numbers if you make a copy of Tables 8.2 through 8.4.

The numbers have been collected:

- To provide you with a good estimate of option prices you may encounter in the marketplace

- To show you how option premiums change under varying conditions

- To allow you to make easy comparisons and better understand how to select an option to sell

The data was generated under these conditions:

- The stock is $60 and pays no dividend

- There are options with 13 weeks and 26 weeks until expiration

37

- Strike prices range from 40 (deep in-the-money) through 80 (far out-of-the-money) in 5-point increments

- The implied volatility[9] is 20, 40, 60, or 90 (the concept of volatility is discussed in Chapter 9)

- The interest rate is 4%

We will use the numbers to make comparisons and draw general conclusions. These conclusions will carry over to your investments and can help you select specific options to sell against your stock holdings. There is a great deal of data in the tables, but you will see it is easy to follow the discussion.

We discuss conclusions related to volatility in chapter 9. We discuss conclusions related to selecting specific options to sell in Chapter 10.

The tables of data

Table 8.1 lists four stocks that trade at each of the four volatility levels used in our discussion. The purpose is to show the type of stocks that typically trade at each of those levels. **Historical volatility** is a property describing the stock and is the actual volatility at

---

[9] Volatility can be described as the tendency of a stock to rise or fall by a significant amount over a short period of time. The **implied volatility** is the marketplace's estimate of future volatility.

which the stock has traded in the past. Over time, you can expect the historical volatility of the stock will gradually change, as the individual companies change. In general, the larger, more solid companies trade with a lower volatility than newer, smaller, faster-growing companies.

Table 8.1
Examples of Stocks With Certain Historical
Volatilities

Historical Volatility	Stock Name
20	Coca Cola Exxon-Mobil H. J. Heinz Johnson & Johnson
40	Alcoa Ford Home Depot Microsoft
60	E*Trade Gap Stores Hewlett Packard Motorola
90	Advanced Fibre Communications Broadcom JDS Uniphase Rational Software

Implied volatility[10] is a property describing the options and is a measure of the <u>estimated</u> future volatility of the stock. It changes over time as the historical volatility of the company changes. It also changes under various conditions, such as market uncertainty, and company specific events, such as earnings reports.

Over time, the average implied volatility of the options approximates the actual historical volatility of the stock. At any given time, the implied volatility may be very different from the average historical volatility. Thus, when you sell call options, you sometimes receive very high prices (when the implied volatility is high) and sometimes the prices are much lower (low implied volatility).

A volatility of 20 is low, and stocks trading at a 20 historical volatility do not move much in a short period of time. Thus, when the options trade with an implied volatility near 20, the premium you receive for selling a call is low, and covered call writing provides only a modest return. However, it may make sense for a very conservative investor to own these stocks. If you already own similar stocks, selling options can increase the annual return by enough to make the strategy worthwhile. The stocks listed in Table 8.1, as representative of 20 volatility stocks, are all of large companies.

---

[10] See footnote 9.

Under extreme conditions, both historical (measured over a short period of time) and implied volatility levels have climbed over 200. However, a volatility of 90 is very high and option prices for such stocks are accordingly high. They are high for a reason.[11] Do not believe there is a guaranteed profit available from selling a covered call on these high volatility stocks. But, if you want to own a high volatility stock, and are comfortable with such a stock in your portfolio, you will love the high potential profits that are available from selling the calls. The companies listed in Table 8.1 with a 90 historical volatility are (at the time this is written) all high-flyer NASDAQ stocks.

Before a description of the numbers in the other tables, a definition:

> **Time value** - The portion of the value of an option that is NOT the intrinsic value. Both the volatility of the underlying stock and the amount of time remaining in the life of the option contribute to the time value. The premium of an out-of-the-money option is entirely its time value.

In order to give you a good estimate of the premium available to you when you begin your program of writing covered call options, Tables 8.2 through 8.4 contain data for a generic $60 stock (no dividend) under a variety of conditions. The six tables contain

---

[11] These stocks really are volatile, and often make significant moves, both up and down. There is a real risk of losing money when you own high volatility stocks, even with the protection that comes with the selling of a call.

data showing the theoretical values (Tables 8.2a and b) for such a stock, the time value of those options (Tables 8.3a and b), and the maximum possible profit (Tables 8.4a and b) from each position. The options expiring in 13 weeks are in Tables 8.2a thru 8.4a, and options expiring in 26 weeks are in Tables 8.2b through 8.4b. Values are shown for stocks trading with an implied volatility of 20, 40, 60, or 90. These numbers are illustrative, as it is unlikely the stock you choose will be exactly 60 or have an implied volatility exactly equal to one of the sample numbers.

The theoretical values of the options listed in Table 8.2 are calculated using a sophisticated mathematical model.[12]

Table 8.3 lists the time value (theoretical value less the intrinsic value, if any) for the same options. These are important numbers because the time value represents the potential profit of an in-the-money option (see Appendix B for why this is true).

Table 8.4 shows the percentage return on your investment, if

- The position is held until expiration, and

- You are assigned on the call

---

[12] We will not delve into the mathematics in this volume, but the factors that determine the theoretical value are discussed in chapter 7.

It is not likely that options that are currently far out-of-the-money will become in-the-money options by the time expiration arrives, but the data in Table 8.4 is based on that assumption for illustrative purposes. (Don't base your investment decision on the expectation that an option that is currently out-of-the-money will be in-the-money at expiration. It may happen, but don't count on it.)

You will seldom, if ever, find a real world stock with numbers exactly matching those in these tables, yet this data is useful because it allows you to think about, and compare data for:

- Selling a shorter term (13-week) vs. a longer term (26-week) option

- Selling options that are deep in-the-money, slightly in-the-money, at-the-money, or out-of-the-money.

- Selling options on stocks trading with different volatilities.

In all the tables, there is a blank row after the strike price of 60 to separate the out-of-the-money calls from the other options.

In order to make intelligent investment decisions, it is necessary for you to determine profit potential and maximum possible returns for each investment. By going over the numbers now, you get much needed practice. Remember to include commissions in your calculations. See appendix B, if necessary, for help with the calculations.

Table 8.2a
Theoretical Values for Calls
$60 Stock Price
Strike Price vs. Implied Volatility
13 Weeks To Expiration

Volatility ➜ Strike ↓	20	40	60	90
40	20.39	20.45	20.90	22.40
45	15.44	15.73	16.70	18.86
50	10.54	11.43	13.00	15.77
55	6.02	7.81	9.88	13.08
60	2.65	4.99	7.33	10.79
65	0.86	3.03	5.37	8.89
70	0.20	1.73	3.83	7.29
75	0.03	0.94	2.73	5.98
80	0.00	0.49	1.90	4.90

Table 8.2b
Theoretical Values for Calls
$60 Stock Price
Strike Price vs. Implied Volatility
26 Weeks To Expiration

Volatility ➜ Strike ▼	20	40	60	90
40	20.78	21.16	22.44	25.26
45	15.91	16.87	18.78	22.31
50	11.23	13.08	15.61	19.70
55	7.11	9.86	12.86	17.38
60	3.94	7.24	10.51	15.32
65	1.92	5.22	8.58	13.58
70	0.81	3.68	6.96	12.03
75	0.30	2.55	5.63	10.61
80	0.10	1.73	4.53	9.44

Mark D. Wolfinger

Table 8.3a
Time Values[13] of the Call Options
$60 Stock
Data From Table 8.2a
Strike Price vs. Implied Volatility
13 Weeks To Expiration

Volatility → Strike ↓	20	40	60	90
40	0.39	0.45	0.90	2.40
45	0.44	0.73	1.70	3.86
50	0.54	1.43	3.00	5.77
55	1.02	2.81	4.88	8.08
60	2.65	4.99	7.33	10.79
65	0.86	3.03	5.37	8.89
70	0.20	1.73	3.83	7.29
75	0.03	0.94	2.73	5.98
80	0.00	0.49	1.90	4.90

[13] **Time Value** is the amount of the option premium that is NOT intrinsic value. Time value = premium less intrinsic value, if any

46

Table 8.3b
Time Values[14] of the Call Options
$60 Stock
Data From Table 8.2b
Strike Price vs. Implied Volatility
26 Weeks To Expiration

Volatility ➜ Strike ▼	20	40	60	90
40	0.78	1.16	2.44	5.26
45	0.91	1.87	3.78	7.31
50	1.23	3.08	5.61	9.70
55	2.11	4.86	7.86	12.38
60	3.94	7.24	10.51	15.32
65	1.92	5.22	8.58	13.58
70	0.81	3.68	6.96	12.03
75	0.30	2.55	5.63	10.61
80	0.10	1.73	4.53	9.44

---

[14] **Time Value** is the amount of the option premium that is NOT intrinsic value. Time value = premium less intrinsic value, if any.

Table 8.4a
% Profit, if Assigned at Expiration
Data From Table 8.2a
Strike Price vs. Implied Volatility
13 Weeks To Expiration

Volatility → Strike ↓	20	40	60	90
40	0.98	1.14	2.30	6.38
45	0.99	1.65	3.93	9.16
50	1.09	2.94	6.38	13.05
55	1.89	5.38	9.74	17.22
60	4.62	9.07	13.92	21.93
65	9.91	14.10	18.98	27.18
70	17.06	20.13	24.62	32.80
75	25.06	26.99	30.91	38.84
80	33.33	34.43	37.69	45.19

Table 8.4b
% Profit, if Assigned at Expiration
Data From Table 8.2b
Strike Price vs. Implied Volatility
26 Weeks To Expiration

Volatility → Strike ↓	20	40	60	90
40	1.99	2.99	6.50	9.61
45	2.06	4.34	8.55	15.33
50	2.52	6.50	12.64	19.28
55	3.99	9.69	16.67	29.05
60	7.03	13.72	21.24	34.29
65	11.91	18.66	26.41	40.03
70	18.26	24.28	31.98	45.92
75	25.63	30.55	37.94	51.85
80	33.56	37.29	44.22	58.23

Chapter 9
Volatility

Volatility can be described as the tendency of a stock to rise or fall by a significant amount over a short period of time. It is measured by tracking the daily price changes, as a <u>percentage</u>, the stock has made in the past. The measurement is from one day's closing price to the next day's closing price. A stock that averages a large percentage daily change has a high volatility. Companies whose stocks tend to be more volatile are in high growth industries and are newer and faster growing. Companies that pay big dividends, are in stable industries, and are older and well-established trade with lower volatility.

If a stock has a volatility of 40, it means that the price has changed by no more than 40% (either up or down) in a year, approximately two out of every three years. A move of twice that size occurs about once every 20 years.

When dealing with stocks, we are not usually interested in the expected price range over a year, but are more concerned with daily changes. The expectation for the daily price change of a stock with a 40% volatility is 2.52% or less (a **one standard deviation move**[15]) approximately two days out of

---

[15] See Appendix B for calculations, and Appendix A for the definition

three. A move of twice that amount (in this case 4.54%) occurs no more than 5% of the time.

Option premium is dependent on implied volatility[16]

When you trade an option, most of the factors used in the calculation of the theoretical value (see Chapter 7) are known. The current stock price, strike price, interest rate, dividend, and time remaining are known. The volatility can only be estimated. The past volatility of the stock can be used as a guide to the future, but what we want to use when calculating the theoretical value of an option is the volatility of the stock from now until the option expires. This can only be estimated. Opinions of future volatility differ. Thus, some buy options thinking they are priced lower than their theoretical value, and others are eager sellers believing they are priced too high. This difference of opinion keeps the markets interesting.

Volatility is truly the major determining factor in the price you receive when selling an option. There is a large difference in the premium of an option when the underlying stock is very volatile, compared with when the stock is stodgy, safe and non-volatile. Stocks that commonly have large price movements have options with correspondingly large premiums.

---

[16] The **implied volatility** is that volatility, that when substituted into the equation for calculating theoretical values, makes the theoretical value equal to the actual price of the option in the marketplace.

What you can discover from the data. Part 1

A careful study of Tables 8.2, 8.3, and 8.4 provides you with much to think about. Some of this discussion is postponed until chapter 10, but below are *some* of the situations that I want to be certain you notice. You will make additional discoveries on your own, as you study the numbers.

1) The effect of changing volatility, is HUGE. Look at the strike price of 80 for a 26-week option in Table 8.2b. A stock with a 20 volatility has very little, if any, chance of climbing from the current 60 to 80, and the call is worth $10. In contrast, for a stock with a 90 volatility, the option is worth $944, as there is a real chance the stock could climb well beyond 80.

2) Selling options that are deep in-the-money[17] does not offer much profit potential when the implied volatility is low. If you want the extra protection that comes with selling a deep in-the-money option, (20 points in-the-money or a 40 strike price in this example), check Table 8.4. It demonstrates that you can earn a decent return of 9.61%

---

[17] **Deep in-the-money** means that the stock price is in-the-money by a large amount, often more than one strike price. In this example, a strike price of 60 is at-the-money; the 55 call is in-the-money, and the calls with strikes of 50 and below are deep in-the-money.

for a 90 volatility stock, but the return is less than 2% for a 20 volatility stock.

3) If your goal is to find an option that allows you to make a predetermined, specific percentage return from your investment (Table 8.4)

   o You can get that return from a high volatility stock by selling a call that is deeper in-the-money when compared with a stock with a lower volatility.

   o To get that same return from a lower volatility stock, you may have to sell a call that is not in-the-money.

The high volatility stock affords greater protection to the downside (because the option is deeper in-the-money). The lower volatility stock offers a different type of protection: it is less likely to make a big downside move. Choose an option with risk characteristics that make you comfortable (more on this topic in the next chapter).

The option values used were derived from a complex mathematical formula. If you prefer to use true option prices from today's market, see chapter 16 to find where you can get option quotes.

You are ready to learn which call option to sell. More conclusions from the tables are in Chapter 10.

Chapter 10
Which Call Option Do You Sell?

You are ready to begin selling covered call options on some, or all, of the stocks in your portfolio. There are decisions to be made.

These are the steps to take:

1. Choose which stocks to include in the covered call writing program. Do you want to sell calls on all, some, or none?

2. Choose the strike and expiration.

   a. Every stock has at least two strike prices, and new strike prices are added as needed (if the price of the stock moves through one strike price, another is added), to ensure there is at least one call and one put that is out-of-the-money.

   b. There is a choice of four expiration months (LEAPS, longer-term options, are discussed separately in Chapter 14).

How do you select the specific call option to sell?

There is no single best option to sell. Each investor must decide the most important objective for each of his stock positions. In some cases, where preservation of capital is most important, your goal is extra safety. With other stocks, you may be inclined to be aggressive and seek additional profits at the expense of some of that safety. The choice is always between extra safety and extra profit potential. Over a period of time, you will probably choose a variety of strategies.

Before you make this decision:

> ❖ **Please remember why you are considering a call writing program in the first place**. It is a conservative method for increasing the amount of money you earn. If you start taking risks, the reason for using call options has vanished. <u>The purpose of this book is to show you how to remain conservative, and still earn significant amounts of money.</u>

Conservative or aggressive options strategy?

The major factor in labeling a covered call position as *conservative* is that it has a reasonable amount of insurance against losing money in the event the stock declines in price. Keep in mind, there is never enough protection in the event of a real debacle. If you almost never take a loss on any of your positions, if your stocks always rise in price, then you are an exceptional picker of stocks and may not have to be conservative. But, if you are like the rest of us, and own stocks that either sit unchanged for long periods of time, or go down in price, then safety should be a welcome addition to your portfolio. This is especially true when that safety comes with sufficient profit potential to attract your attention. Our major goal is still making money, but it is reassuring to know that we are making money and being safer at the same time.

To repeat, the purpose of this book is to teach you a conservative options strategy. When you begin to look for options to sell, not all the choices result in a safe, conservative position. It is necessary to describe the different choices and the risks associated with those choices. I cannot overemphasize that I've included them for the sake of completeness, and that I strongly urge you to adopt the conservative approach.

In general, conservative choice is an option with a high premium. The *aggressive* choice is an option with a lower premium, but with the opportunity to make more dollars over a given period of time.

If you choose the conservative route, you will select a longer-term option that is slightly in-the-money. We take a detailed look at selling this type of call later in the chapter. This choice is best any time preservation of capital is your main objective. This occurs when you are bearish on the stock market, when you are nearing retirement and want to avoid capital loss, when you will need substantial capital for another purpose in the not-too-distant future, or at any time that safety is paramount. Once again, this is the strategy that I recommend, especially as you begin using options. This investment style affords <u>substantial potential for profit</u>, and you may never be tempted to take more risk. I truly hope that turns out to be the case, because

<u>I am writing this book to teach you how to make more money, not how to take risk.</u>

Depending on the stocks you own, there is an excellent chance to increase earnings by at least 20% per year. <u>There is no need to take substantial risk if returns of that magnitude are available at lower risk!</u> I know other authors promise much higher returns. Those returns are available to you also, but only if you accept more risk.

If you are inclined to do so, there is time to get more aggressive after you gain some experience with options. The aggressive and more risky strategies that allow the potential for greater profits involve selling options with shorter expirations, and/or options that are out-of-the-money. These covered call positions offer less downside protection because you receive less premium when you sell the call option. If you sell out-of-the-money calls, in return for accepting a smaller premium, you have the chance to make additional profit if your stock rises in price. (When assigned you must sell your stock for the strike price, so if you sell a call with a higher strike price, there is a *possibility* of selling the stock at a higher price.) When we discuss Table 10.1 later in this chapter, we compare safer vs. more aggressive positions.

If you accept less protection by selling options with shorter expirations, you may be able to collect more total premium dollars over time (even though you collect less per option sold, you sell more options for more total dollars over the course of the year). Do not forget to include the cost of commissions in your calculations, since more trades means more commissions.

If you choose to adopt either of these more aggressive approaches, I recommend that you do not use it as your only options strategy. An aggressive approach is appropriate when you are bullish on the stock market or when you are more interested in capital gains than in preservation of capital.

Message One to the buy and hold investor

Even though I want to encourage you, as a buy and hold investor, to seriously consider adopting the conservative approach to writing covered calls, I recognize that selling out-of-the-money options might have more appeal to you. When you buy stocks, you seek capital gains. Selling out-of-the-money calls provides the opportunity to collect a premium from the sale of options, while you still maintain your traditional investment goal of seeking capital gains.

A more conservative option strategy minimizes losses when the markets turn against you, and still allows you to make good money when your stocks go up. Sometimes the resulting profit is less than you would have made without the sale of the option, but sometimes the conservative approach provides a nice cushion if your stocks either decline in price, or are relatively unchanged. Nonetheless, if you, as a buy and hold investor, want to enter the option market in a gradual way, selling out-of-the-money calls is a reasonable way to begin. In my opinion, it is not the best way, it is not the safest way, it is not the recommended way to take advantage of the opportunities available from the intelligent use of stock options, but it is a good way to begin your options education.

The more conservative positions

The price of an option (premium) is composed of two parts:

Premium = Intrinsic Value + Time Value

The intrinsic value of the option is defined as the amount that the option is in-the-money.[18]

The time value of an option is the portion of the premium derived from the volatility and time remaining. It is the part of the premium that is not intrinsic value.

If an option is out-of-the-money, the entire premium is the **time value** of the option (intrinsic value is zero). When an option is in-the-money, the premium is composed of an intrinsic value and a time value, per the above equation.

When you sell an option that has an intrinsic value:

---

[18] See glossary, Appendix A. Intrinsic value of a call is the amount that the stock price exceeds the strike price. See Appendix B (if necessary) to see how the intrinsic value is calculated.

- The higher premium you receive provides additional protection against a decrease in the stock price. You can think of selling an in-the-money option as receiving a refund (of the intrinsic value) of part of your purchase price for that investment, in addition to receiving time value for the option. Do not look at it as selling someone the right to buy your stock for less than you paid for it, but rather as simply getting a refund of part of your investment.

- The time value of the option is your potential profit.[19]

Higher premium in the option you sell makes for a more conservative position. Options with longer expirations are somewhat conservative; in-the-money options are more conservative.

In summary, selling an in-the-money option:

- Provides more protection because you receive a higher premium for the sale

- Reduces the maximum profit potential because

  o There is less time value in the option. In-the-money options have less time

---

[19] See Appendix B if you are not sure why this is true.

value than at-the-money options (Table 8.3).

o   There is no opportunity for additional profit from an increase in the price of the stock

Since your potential profit for an in-the-money call depends on the time value of the option you sell, you cannot sell just any in-the-money option. Some deep in-the-money calls have little time value hence little profit potential. Use your judgment and balance the profit potential with the downside protection, and choose an option that results in a position that is most comfortable for you. This is not as difficult as it sounds, and there is no right answer. In fact, you might easily select one strategy for a given stock, and then select a different strategy the next time that you sell an option for the same stock.

Covered call writing is not purely a science; as there is a good deal of personal judgment involved. Sometimes you are aggressive and seek a higher potential profit and at other times you settle for a smaller profit to gain additional safety.

In discussing different strategies, it is more meaningful to look at real numbers. Referring back to tables 8.2 thru 8.4 in chapter 8, it is time to draw some additional conclusions:

What you can discover from the data. Part 2

<u>This example is very important</u>. It contains the basis of the assertion that a conservative approach provides safety for your portfolio as well as the opportunity for significant profits.

A) Let's look at a conservative approach. Finding the data in Tables 8.2b, consider what happens if your stock is $60 per share, trading with a volatility of 60, and you sell the option that is:

- A long term (26 week) call

- In-the-money, with a strike price of 55

    o You sell the call for 12.86 (Table 8.2b)

    o Your maximum return is 16.67% (Table 8.4b). Your investment is 47.14 (the 60 stock price less the 12.86 premium you receive). The profit potential is 7.86 (the time value).

Original Investment	$6000
Less Option Premium	-$1286
Net Investment	$4714

Maximum Return = Maximum Profit ÷ Net Investment

Maximum Return = $786 ÷ $4714 = 16.67%

> o You are protected if your stock declines 12.86 points (the amount you collect from the sale of the call), or 21.43% of the current price.

Call Premium Collected ÷ Original Investment = Protection

$1286 ÷ $6000 = 21.43%

Let's assume you already own this particular stock, so your choices are:

- Hold the stock and do not sell the call

- Hold the stock and sell the call

If you do not sell the call:

- To make the same return (16.67%) in six months, the stock must appreciate from 60 to 70

- You have no protection to the downside. A decline in the stock price results in a loss

- There is no limit to your potential profit

Compare the two strategies:

To make 16.67% in six months:

- With the buy and hold strategy, the stock must rise to 70

- With the covered call strategy, the stock must stay above 55

Which is a more likely occurrence? Clearly, there is a much greater chance the stock will be 55 or higher than 70 or higher at expiration.[20] Thus, there is a much better chance to make a 16.67% profit by choosing to sell the call option. However, with the call option strategy, that is the most you can make. If you do not sell the call, it is possible to make an unlimited amount. Thus, the choice: do you want the much more likely return (in this example it is 16.67%) or the opportunity to make an unlimited amount? For me, it is an easy choice. I love those solid, returns again and again.

But wait; there is another important point to be made. If you adopt the buy and hold strategy, you lose money if the stock declines in price. With the option strategy, you do not lose any money unless the stock declines by more than 21.43%. That is a lot of insurance. Isn't it worth giving up the chance to make more than 16.67% in return for receiving that insurance - especially when it is coupled with the increased probability that you will make 16.67%?

---

[20] Every time the stock is above 70, it is also above 55. Thus, the chance the stock will close above 55 includes **all** of the time that it is above 70, plus the time it finishes between 55 and 70.

The Bottom Line: In exchange for giving up the chance to make more in the event the stock makes a large advance in price, you receive

- Good protection in case the stock goes down

- A higher probability of making the predetermined profit. You make this profit, even if the stock does not go up. In fact you make the maximum profit if the stock declines (in this case, by 5 points) to the strike price

This demonstrates why this type of position is considered very conservative. It gives you protection against a loss plus a good chance for a healthy profit. And what does it cost for that insurance and likely profit? - the chance to make a bonanza on the stock.

Again, it is your money and your decision, but I prefer the extra safety coupled with the likelihood of a substantial return on my investment. <u>Be sure that you understand the concept of the above discussion, for it is the heart of the argument in favor of adopting a conservative covered call writing strategy.</u>

B) Other conclusions from the data in tables 8.2 through 8.4:

1. If you sell an in-the-money call, as you choose lower and lower strike prices (the options become more in-the-money), you

receive less time premium, but more protection (Table 8.3)

2. If you sell an out-of-the-money call, as you choose higher and higher strike prices, you receive less time premium and less protection (Table 8.3)

3. In a strong, rising market, the maximum possible gains come from selling out-of-the-money calls (Table 8.4) - **BUT** this is based on the assumption that the stock rises above the strike price and the option is assigned. That assumption is made for illustrative purposes; you will be disappointed if you expect it to happen often in the real world. Selling the (slightly) in-the-money option is a safer strategy

4. Let's compare the sale of the 26-week option with the sale of the 13-week option:

   • The long-term option has more premium, affording greater safety

   • The short-term option provides more premium dollars *per month*. In return for less protection, there is the *chance* to make more dollars over the course of a year

- Over the period of 26 weeks, you can sell one longer-term option *or* two of the shorter-term options (one now, then another after the first expires). The price you get for the sale of the second 13-week call is unknown, for that occurs in the future. The price available depends on the stock price and implied volatility at that time

- Do not ignore commissions. They are a significant expense, especially if you sell options more often

5. These tables contain a lot of information. Please take the time to digest the numbers and think about how best to achieve your investment goals. Each stock in your portfolio may require a slightly different strategy

6. There is always a balance between a higher potential return and a higher risk

The point of the discussion is once you have selected the stock, you have a choice of calls to sell, and that choice depends on how conservative you want to be. You may feel bullish or bearish for the next three to six months, and allow that to dictate your strategy. If you prefer to unload a particular stock from your portfolio, then sell a call that is in-the-money, because it is more likely to be assigned[21] at expiration, allowing you to sell the stock. If you prefer to keep the stock, then sell an out-of-the-money call, as it is less likely to finish in-the-money (when compared with a call that is already in-the-money), and you may not be assigned at expiration. There are so many factors that go into making the decision that more than one call could be an acceptable choice. Choose the option that fits your comfort level. Although it is wonderful to increase your annual return by a large amount, it is satisfying to know that a conservative approach can provide you with substantial additional income.

Message Two to the buy and hold investor

We saw how well the conservative strategy works when we sold the longer-term in-the-money option, specifically the 26-week, 55-strike call.

If you, as a buy and hold investor, are primarily interested in making a profit based on your stock going up in price, and are not yet convinced to adopt the more conservative approach when selecting which covered call to sell, then let's look at an example that is more suitable for you at this time. Under identical circumstances, with the stock priced at 60, let's compare selling the 26-week, 55-strike call with selling the 26-week, 70-strike call. All of the data used in the following discussion is either directly from, or calculated from, Tables 8.2-8.4.

---

[21] Since the option is already in-the-money, there is a greater chance it will finish in-the-money when compared with an option that is currently out-of-the-money.

Let's look at Table 10.1, and compare selling a 10 points out-of-the-money call vs. selling a 5 points in-the-money call. You receive almost $600 less (696 vs. 1286) cash for the 70 call than for the 55 call and have less protection against a decline in the price of the stock. You are still protected against a decline of 11.6%, which is a substantial amount, but that is about half the protection available from the sale of the 55 call (21.43%).

Table 10.1
Compare Covered Call Positions. $60 Stock
Data from Tables 8.2b-8.4b

↓ Property/Strike Price →	55 Call	70 Call
Option Premium	1286	696
Time Value of Option	786	696
No Loss if Stock Drops to	47.14	53.04
No Loss if Stock Drops	21.43%	11.60%
Max Profit (Assigned)	16.67%	31.98 %
Profit If Stock Is 60 at Exp	16.67%	13.12%
Profit If Stock Is 55 at Exp	16.67%	3.70%
Profit If Stock Is 50 at Exp	6.07%	(5.73%)

Let's consider expiration possibilities (Table 10.1):

If the stock is unchanged at expiration, the profits are similar, but the edge goes to the more conservative strategy. Selling the 55-strike call results in a gain of $786, or 16.67%. Selling the 70-strike call results in a gain of $696 or 13.12%. Note that the profit in each case is the time value of the option.

If the stock declines by 5 points (from 60 to 55) during the lifetime of the option, the more conservative strategy is the clear winner. If the stock is 55 at expiration, the writer of the 55 call still makes his maximum possible profit of 16.67% ($786 on an investment of $4714). The writer of the 70 call loses $500 on the decline in the price of his stock, but makes $696 from the sale of the call, for a profit of 3.70% ($196 on an investment of $5304).

If the stock drops all the way to 50 at expiration, the conservative strategy still affords a profit of $286 (6.06%; loss of $1000 on the stock and a gain of $1286 on the call) and the more aggressive strategy results in a loss of $304 (5.73%; the loss is $1000 on the stock, but the gain is $696 from the call).

The biggest difference between the two strategies appears in the event that the stock has a significant rally. If the stock rises to 70 or higher, the more conservative position returns its maximum of 16.67% ($786 on an investment of $4714) and the more aggressive position returns a profit of $1000 on the stock, plus the call premium of $696. That is a return of 31.98% ($1696 on an investment of $5304). In this scenario, the aggressive strategy is the clear winner.

These results demonstrate the difference between the conservative and aggressive strategies. The investor who is more concerned with safety, and sells an in-the-money call does better when the price of the stock declines or is relatively unchanged. That fits his objectives of:

- Good profit if stock increases in price

- Good profit if stock declines by a small amount or is unchanged

- Protection against a decline in the stock price

The aggressive investor is more concerned with capital gains than with safety. He sells an out-of-the-money call and does best if the stock rises in price. That fits his objectives of:

- Making money from an increase in the price of the stock

- Still showing a profit if the stock is unchanged

- Accepting less protection against a decline in the price of the stock in return for the chance to do better when the stock goes up

This example illustrates how an investor who chooses the more conservative strategy can make money more often, and lose money less often than the investor who accepts more risk. You, as the buy and hold investor, have always earned your profits from owning stocks that have gone up in price. You can continue that

71

investment style by writing (selling) out-of-the-money options against your long stock positions. If you switch at least a portion of your portfolio to a more conservative strategy, you will be able to earn money even when your stocks do not perform well. Your choice is between more safety coupled with good profits, and less safety and the *chance* to make more money.

You also have a compromise choice. In the above example, a slightly more conservative action is to sell the 65-strike call instead of the 70 call. You still sell an out-of-the-money call, but one with more protection and less upside profit potential. You can also consider selling the at-the-money 60 call. In short, these are all reasonable choices and the decision is yours.

After the call sale, then what?

Once you make your selection and sell the call, it becomes time to relax. I repeat for emphasis, it is time to relax. Time is working on your side.[22] Don't ignore your positions, but there is no need to fret over them. If you are currently a buy and hold investor who seldom reviews his positions, then I suggest you take the opportunity to review your positions every month when your statement arrives. It is always a good idea to know which stocks you really want to own, and which you are willing to sell. Since you will be

---

[22] An option is a wasting asset. That means the time value of the option decays every day. (The intrinsic value depends on the price of the stock, and can go either up or down.). Since you sold the option, you benefit from that time decay.

generating additional cash from the periodic sale of call options, as well as from being assigned on some options, you will have money for future investments. It is a good idea to keep an eye open for stocks you want to buy.

When expiration day is approaching, it is time to watch your positions more closely. As expiration nears, you may decide to make a change, rather than wait for the option to expire. This concept is discussed in more detail in chapter 11.

Another caution. When you sold the call, you had a particular profit potential in mind. Don't make a beginner's error of rushing back into the marketplace to buy back the option (at a loss) you sold, because the stock makes a rally. Keep in mind if the stock goes higher, that is good for you. The higher the stock, the more likely the call will be assigned at expiration, and the greater the probability you make the maximum profit on your position. <u>Making your profit objective is the best that you can do with the position, so be happy if you make it</u>, and do not be concerned if, on occasion, you might have made more without the call sale. Some inexperienced investors mistakenly feel if they sell a call option and the stock rises, they have lost money. That is not the case. The decision has been made to sell the stock at a specific price for a specific profit. If you make that profit, be glad. You have a real profit, not a loss.

What if you don't own stock? What if your stock doesn't have listed options?

A different thought pattern is required when you do not already own the stock. You can buy the stock and sell the call at the same time. This is a **buy-write transaction**. (Selling a covered call is sometimes referred to as writing the call.) When you do this, you have two objectives in mind:

- First, and most importantly, you are making a new investment in a stock. Be certain it is the stock of a company you want to own. *I offer no instruction on how to make a stock market investment. I offer this advice: buy a stock you want to own.* In our previous discussion, you already owned the stock. Under those conditions, your choice was whether or not to sell the call, and then which call to sell. Here you are making a new investment, and it may be tempting to enter into a buy-write transaction simply because a given stock has a very high option premium. This is a dangerous strategy. The reward potential may be high, but it is not a good idea to invest your money in a company unless you are comfortable owning its stock. One of the main arguments in favor of selling covered calls is that it is a very profitable, conservative investment technique. It is more foolhardy than conservative to take a position in a stock that you do not really *want* to own, just because there is a large possible gain from a buy-write position.

- Second, when you invest in a new stock, you must consider if the premium available from the sale of a call is high enough to earn the investment return you want. If these conditions are not satisfied, then you have three choices:

   o Buy this stock without selling a call

   o Invest the money elsewhere for now and wait for another opportunity

   o Buy the stock and sell the option, accepting a lower rate of return

If you love the stock, go ahead and buy it. It is not necessary that you sell a call against every position.

Options are available for many stocks. However, there are some that do not have listed options. It is okay to invest in those companies, but you have to forego the opportunity to write covered calls.

As you can see, this is not an exact science. Your emotions come into play. Your feeling on how conservative or aggressive you want to be comes into play. You decide the amount of premium you are willing to accept for relinquishing the right to participate in a large increase in your stock price. After you go through the decision-making process a few times, you will have a better understanding of how to put all the decisions together and select an appropriate call option to sell. Different people come to different conclusions, based upon the individual decision-making process.

Chapter 11

Rolling The Position

When you hold a covered call position, it is advantageous to wait for expiration (the third Friday of the month). If you are assigned, (this occurs when the call you sold finishes[23] in-the-money) you make the maximum amount your position allows. You must pay a commission if you are assigned and sell the stock. There is no commission if the call expires worthless.

Despite the desirability of waiting, there will be times when you want to manage the position. That means you want to trade, or modify your position prior to expiration. You do this:

- When the risk of the position is increasing due to a stock price decline

- When a temporary profit opportunity is present

One method of managing the position is simply to buy the call you previously sold. You might do this if the call reached a low price and there was still a reasonable amount of time until expiration.

---

[23] Finishes refers to the stock price at the close of business on expiration day.

Most of the time you manage the position by making two trades: a) buy back the option you sold earlier and b) sell another call option with a more distant expiration date. This type of trade is called **rolling**. Sometimes the trade is defensive, and you do it to gain additional insurance against a further decline in the stock. At other times you want to take advantage of a profit opportunity that is present now, but which may no longer be available after expiration.

Rolling as a defensive move

If you have a covered call position, the stock has moved down in price and time has passed, then the option you sold is no longer offering much protection against a further decline in the stock price. You have two basic choices in this situation:

- Do nothing. Wait for expiration. At that time you can decide which, if any, option to sell

- Buy back the option you previously sold, and sell another option for additional cash, and additional downside protection

Example

You own a stock trading at 38, and sell a six-month call with a strike price of 40. You collect a premium of 4.

Your maximum risk in this position is $3400 (if the stock declines all the way to zero).

Assume four months have passed and the stock has fallen to 32. While you are not happy the stock is down so much, you are glad you sold the call option, for it has reduced your loss.

If you believe

- The stock will recover

- You are happy to hold the stock at the current price

- You don't need additional insurance

then there is no need for any action on your part. You simply wait. This is not entirely consistent with a conservative approach to covered call writing, but it is your money and your decision.

However, if you are concerned the stock has risk of a further price decline, you can roll the position to gain additional protection. This decision is consistent with the conservative strategy.

To gain additional protection, buy the option you sold earlier. In our example, there are two months until the option expires, and it is 8 points out-of-the-money (strike 40; stock 32). It will not be a very expensive option. The option price depends on many market factors, but for this example, assume that you can buy it for 0.70 ($70 per contract).

At the same time[24] you buy that option, sell a new option with an additional six months until expiration. You can sell the call with the same strike price of 40, but since you are most interested in preservation of capital, you would probably sell the option with the strike price of 35 instead. A reasonable price for this option (depending on many market variables) is 4.70. If you pay 0.7 and collect 4.70, you receive additional option premium of 4.00 ($400, less commissions). The amount you have invested in the position has been reduced from $3400 to $3000. You can no longer sell your stock for 40, but may be obligated to sell it for 35.

What happened? You gave up something to gain the additional protection. You gave up the opportunity to sell the stock at your original 40 price target. But look at it this way: you owned the stock at 38. If you used the buy and hold strategy, you would have a current loss of $600, since the stock has dropped by 6 points. Instead, you sold calls twice on this position, taking in a total premium of $800. Thus, you have a stock that is 32 and your cost is 30, instead of 38. This is a much better situation than you would be in without the call sales. Imagine - you have a potential profit (if the

---

[24] By telling your broker you want to do a **spread transaction** at a limit price (the premium you collect less the premium you pay), he will place the order so that both trades are executed at the same time. If the broker is unable to do both parts of the trade, then neither will be executed. You can re-enter the order with a different limit price, or wait and hope for your price.

stock is above 30 at expiration) on a stock that has
declined 6 points!

If the stock rises and you are later assigned on the call
option (at 35 per share), then your profit is the $3500
you receive for the sale, less your revised cost of
$3000, or $500. This is less than the $600 profit goal
you had when you sold the first call option, but just
having a profit is a good result since you own a stock
that declined in price.

Rolling for opportunity

You maximize profits and minimize expenses by
waiting until expiration, but sometimes there are
reasons for rolling before expiration.

> 1) Consider rolling early if option prices are
> especially high, due to an increased **implied
> volatility**.[25] In this scenario, buy back your
> soon-to-expire option and sell, in a spread
> transaction,[26] a call with an additional six
> months until expiration. By making the
> trade early, you lock in a good price. Your
> goal in rolling is to collect enough cash to
> make it desirable to hold the position.

---

[25] The implied volatility is a measure of how the marketplace
estimates the future price movement in the stock. A high implied
volatility often occurs when a news event is imminent or when the
entire market is at a crossroads.

[26] A spread is two simultaneous trades in which you buy one
option and sell another.

Even if premium levels are high, you may not want to roll this position if the net premium available for the spread transaction is less than you want to accept. In that case, wait.

2) The price is too tempting. If you plan to keep the stock and sell a new option with the *same* strike price, it may pay to make the trade early. If the stock makes a significant move, the premium you can collect for selling the time spread will be reduced.[27] By trading early, you can lock in a price that is acceptable to you. However, if the stock remains near the strike price as the days pass, the time spread widens even more and you could get a better price by waiting. Again, not an exact science. The conservative approach is to make the trade when the price (after commissions) makes you want the position for another six months.

3) Your option is in-the-money, and you do not want to sell your stock. The only way to keep the stock is to buy back the option. Buy back the call and sell a new call in a spread transaction. Select the month and strike price as if you are selling an option in this stock for the first time. But, if you do not like the prices available, allow yourself

---

[27] The time spread is worth the most when the stock is very close to the strike price and it is very near to expiration day

to be assigned. After all, you did make the maximum possible for your position, and there is no need to hold this stock if the profit potential is too small. You can reinvest the proceeds from the sale of your stock elsewhere. You may even get another chance later to repurchase the stock at a lower price.

If none of these situations pertain, that is good. Just wait for expiration and start the process again.

Once you have made your decision and rolled the position, it is again time to relax and wait for the next expiration.

Chapter 12
Buy Low; Sell High

Now that you have become familiar with covered call writing and know how to select an option to sell and manage the position, it is time take a different view of the covered call strategy. Options are versatile instruments and can be used in different ways to achieve investment goals. Call options can be used to:

- Sell stock at a higher price

- Buy stock at a lower price

Since you already know how call options work, you can easily assimilate these concepts and add them to your options repertoire. For this discussion, assume you own a stock priced at 30.50. Also assume you receive a premium of 5 for the sale of a 7-month, 30-strike call. When you plan your strategy, please remember to include commissions in your calculations.

Sell stock at higher price

If you want to sell the stock for 35 when it is trading for 30.50, you can place a good 'til cancelled order with your broker to sell the stock for 35. If the stock trades at that price, you will sell it. Decide how likely it is for the stock to reach 35 and how long you are willing to wait for that to happen.

Or you can use the call option described above. If you sell the option for 5 now, all you need to get your 35 price is for the stock to be above 30 in seven months (when the option expires). You will be assigned an exercise notice and sell your stock for 30. Add that to the 5 you received for the call and you sold your stock for 35.

This example illustrates that you have the choice of hoping the stock rises to 35 at any time, or that it will be above 30 when the option expires. It illustrates how you can use a call option to sell stock for more than the current price.

These are two methods for attempting to sell the stock for 35 when it is trading for 30.50. It is your investment and your decision which to try.

Buy stock at a lower price

The stock is trading for 30.50 and you want to buy it for no more than 26. You have two choices. The first is to place a good 'til cancelled order with your broker to buy the stock for 26. As in the previous example, you have to decide how likely it is that you will be able to buy the stock for your price, and how long you are willing to wait.

Or you can use the call option (described above) to achieve your goal. Do a buy-write transaction and buy the stock for 30.5. At the same time, sell the call option for 5. Your net investment for the position is now 25.50. By using the call option, you have achieved your goal of buying the stock for less than your target price of 26. However, for the next seven months, your profit potential is limited. Regardless of how high it goes, you will not be able to sell your stock for more than 30.

If you are eventually assigned and are forced to sell the stock, you have a seven-month profit of $450, or 17.65%. That should be a consolation to you, even if you didn't want to sell the stock.

Thus, the choice: Do you want to buy the stock, write the call, and face the possibility of being forced to sell (for a nice profit) the stock (when assigned on the call), or do you prefer to hope the stock dips in price so you can buy it for 26? Your decision, but the call writing strategy is much more likely to be successful.

If you do choose the buy-write strategy, and time passes and the stock remains near 30, you may have an opportunity to buy back the call you sold. If enough time has passed, and if the stock dips under the strike price, the option may become available for 0.50 or less. If so, you can afford to buy it back. If you add the 0.50 that you pay for the option to the 25.50 you paid for the stock, you have a total cost of 26, your original price target. You own the stock and are under no obligation to sell it. This example illustrates how you can use a call option to buy stock at a lower (than current) price.

Chapter 13

Psychology

The basic covered call writing strategy is successful and produces additional income MOST of the time. If you can accept that you will derive extra income from a high percentage of your option positions and that occasionally you would have done better without an option position, then you are well suited for covered call writing. You will be significantly better off as the time passes and your additional earnings grow.

If you sell a covered call option and see the stock make a large move upwards, how will you react? If you stay calm and truthfully tell yourself that you sold the option with a specific goal in mind and that any stock price increase after that level did not bother you, then you have a winning attitude and are an ideal options candidate.

On the other hand, if you must always have the best of all possible results, then call writing is not for you. If, after making money on a few successful covered call positions, it would upset you or make you angry to see one stock rise through the strike price; if you would feel that selling the call was a mistake and that you would have held the stock and not sold as the stock rose, then you are not a suitable candidate for the covered call approach.

An option writer must have patience to allow time to pass. If you race to buy (for a loss) a call you sold because the stock is going up, this strategy won't work for you. If you understand it is good for you, as the owner of a covered call position, when the stock goes up, then this strategy is for you. If the maximum possible profit from a position is not good enough, and you aren't satisfied that selling the call provided benefits that were not available otherwise, this strategy is not for you.

Remember, those extra benefits include insurance against a drop in the stock price. If the stock price rises, that doesn't alter the fact that insurance was desirable when you made the trade. You have fire insurance on your house, life insurance, and car insurance. Aren't you glad when you do not have to use that insurance? Rooting for your stock to go down because you bought insurance is similar to hoping your house burns down so you can collect on the insurance policy. Insurance is just that - insurance. It is there to protect you, and you hope that you don't have to use it. It is the same in the stock market. You may have insurance against a decline, but you will be better off if the stock goes up. So if the stock goes up, be glad that you will make your profit.

If you are comfortable with a strategy that works well over time, then you will do well. If you are the type of person who benefits from knowing your portfolio is safer, you will also benefit from using the lessons taught in this book. Invest wisely. Protect those investments with covered calls. Rest easy.

Chapter 14

LEAPS

LEAPS, the acronym for Long Term Equity AnticiPation Series, is another type of equity option. These puts and calls have January (always a choice of two years) expirations and expire as far as three years in the future.

Because of the long time until expiration, the premium is relatively large and a covered call position provides a good deal of protection. However, the annualized return is reduced because of the long time until expiration.

I do not recommend using LEAPS options as a vehicle for selling covered calls because

- The annualized rate of return is much lower than with shorter-term options

- It is much more difficult to roll a position when the option has a long time until its expiration

- There is a satisfaction that comes with the successful completion (at expiration) of an option trade. LEAPS provide less opportunity to achieve that feeling. This is a psychological factor, and not related to profit, but it has real value to many investors

Chapter 15

Investment Clubs

An investment club is a group of people bound by a common interest - making investments in the stock market. They meet on a regular basis and discuss topics related to club business. Their most important feature is their careful research of possible investments.

If your club takes the investment business seriously, I recommend your group consider the possibilities of covered call writing. This strategy is a perfect vehicle for a group of investors.

Since you can't sell a call option unless you own at least 100 shares, this strategy is not feasible for clubs that have little money to invest. But, if your club has accumulated assets, or if you collect more than $1000 per month, then you are in a position to study a call writing strategy the same way you research new stocks to buy.

The basic club strategy is to find growth companies that increase in value over time. The concept of selling the right to purchase your stocks to someone else, especially when you have carefully researched which stocks to buy, may feel wrong. However, I suggest you look at new investments in a different way.

By using options, you may be able to collect the 'growth' from the stock much sooner than you had expected.

Consider a scenario in which you have $3800 to invest. The stock of choice is 38 per share, so you want to buy 100 shares. In the traditional investment method, you call your broker and buy the 100 shares for $3800 (plus commission). You now own the stock. If it goes up you make money; if it goes down you lose money.

Consider this as an alternative. Suppose someone tells you that he has 100 shares of stock and he will sell it to you for the discounted price of 34. But, he is not 100% sure that he wants to part with the stock, so in return for giving you that fat discount, there is a stipulation. The stipulation is that in six months he has the right to repurchase the stock from you for 40 per share. If he wants to pay you $4000 for the 100 shares of stock, you are obligated to sell it to him, regardless of the actual market price. If he declines to pay $4000, then the stock is yours free and clear (you own it at the discounted price, and are under no further obligation).

This alternative, as described, is the same as selling a six-month call option with a strike price of 40, for $400.

Which sounds better to you?

- ONE

  You own the stock. You expect to make money as the company grows.

  You make money if the stock goes up; you lose money if the stock goes down.

- TWO

  You own the stock, and saved $400 on the price. That $400 is yours to keep, no matter what happens.

In six months, you might be forced to sell the stock for a profit of $600 (17.65% return, less commissions), collecting the growth quickly.

You cannot sell your stock at a higher price during the next six months, no matter how high it might go.

In comparing the choices:

- Choice ONE is better when the stock is over $44 per share at the end of six months. (You invested $3800. To make the same $600 profit, the stock price must rise to 44.)

- Choice TWO affords a better result:

If the stock price is lower

If the stock is unchanged

If the stock price increases, but is under 44

If the stock is over 40, and the original seller wants to repurchase it, the $600 profit represents a return of 17.65% in six months. Despite the fact that sometimes you might make more, if your club earns money at this rate, it will be wildly successful (Money doubles in just over two years at this rate).

If you do sell your stock (from being assigned on the call) for a profit of over 17% in six months, this is a successful result. In only six months, you captured growth, which is the reason you bought the stock. The growth, of course, may be a result of the option selling strategy, and not directly from stock selection. You are allowed to keep the profit anyway.

Unless your group consists of spectacular stock pickers, most of the time you will be glad you bought the stock for the discounted price. These discounts can make a substantial difference in the performance of your club.

In summary, by using a simple options strategy, you can accomplish this:

- Buy stock at a discount (giving up the possibility of making a killing)

- Insure against a stock price decline

In addition, you are more likely to have a profit after six months (the stock is more likely to be over 34 than it is to be over 38).

Discuss this strategy at your next meeting. It will take an effort to convince others. Be patient. Demonstrate that selling a covered call would have made additional profits for the club on previous purchases. Pass this book on to someone else. Eventually other members will show more interest in options.

Chapter 16

Option Quotes

In Chapter 8, we used table 8.2 to provide theoretical option prices for a stock under specific conditions. We used that data to estimate the actual option premium you would get from selling a call option.

It is better to use real quotes for options you are considering as covered call candidates. It's impossible to call a broker every few minutes to ask for quotes. But if you have access to the Internet, you can have free option quotes! These quotes are slightly delayed, but you will be in position to see the current option premiums available. That makes it possible for you to calculate the protection and profit potential of a trade. So, the question is:

Where do you find option quotes?

Ask your broker if he has a website with option quotes. If not, the options exchanges provide 20-minute delayed quotes. If that is not good enough, you should be able to find a vendor that sells live option quotes. It really isn't necessary to pay for live data. For almost every need, the delayed quotes are sufficient. When you are in the process of making a trade, then the broker should provide live quotes. If not, find a broker who provides that service.

Two of the places where delayed quotes are available:

CBOE:

http://quote.cboe.com/QuoteTable.asp

AMEX:

http://www.amex.com

Chapter 17

Conclusion

At this point I hope you are comfortable discussing options, and are ready to change one of your stock holdings into a covered call position. If you start with the conservative approach, I am confident you will be comfortable with your positions, and pleased with the results.

If that is indeed the case, it's your turn to spread the word and tell someone about the edge that the use of stock options provides. Pass this book along to a friend, or better yet, give them a new copy.

If you have questions, e-mail me and I'll try to give a satisfactory reply. I cannot give investment advice (such as "What stock should I buy?").

mark@mdwoptions.com

I wrote this book hoping more investors become aware of the opportunities available from the conservative use of options.

You can be next to take advantage of this underutilized investment tool.

Appendix A

Glossary

Assigned (an exercise notice) - Notified that the option owner exercised his rights making you obligated to fulfill the terms of the option contract.

At-the-money - An option whose strike price is equal to the price of the underlying asset.

Buy-Write Transaction - The simultaneous purchase of 100 shares of stock and sale of one call option.

Call - An option contract that gives its owner the right to buy the underlying asset at the strike price for a specified time.

Covered Call - A call option that has been sold and is backed by an equivalent number of shares of stock.

Exercise - The election by the owner of an option to do what the option allows: either buy or sell the underlying at the strike price.

Exercise Notice - Notification that the owner of the option has exercised that option. The person assigned this notice is now obligated to fulfill the terms of the contract.

Expiration - The date, after which, the option is no longer a valid contract. For stock options, it is the third Friday of the specified month.

Expire Worthless - What happens to an option if it is out-of-the-money at the close of business on expiration day, and the owner does not exercise it.

Historical Volatility - The volatility of the stock in the past. It is used to estimate the future volatility. Historical volatility is a property of the stock.

Implied volatility - The volatility that, when inserted into the equation for calculating the theoretical value of an option, makes the theoretical value the same as the price of the option in the marketplace. Implied volatility is a property of the option.

In-the-money - A call option with a strike price lower than the price of the underlying asset, or a put option with a strike price higher than that of the underlying. An option with an intrinsic value.

Intrinsic Value - The part of the premium attributed to the fact the option is in-the-money.

LEAPS - Acronym for Long Term Equity AnticiPation Series. Puts and calls with January expirations up to three years in the future.

Long - The position resulting from owning an asset.

Margin - The amount that must be deposited in the account in the form of cash or eligible securities. The deposit is required to protect the broker against the risk of loss.

Margin Account - An account in which an investor buys securities on credit, using other securities held in the account as collateral.

Obligations - Attributes forced upon the seller of an option.

Option - A contract that gives its owner the right, but not the obligation, to either buy or sell a specified underlying asset at a specified price for a specified period of time.

Options Clearing Corporation (OCC) is an organization that keeps records for every outstanding options contract. When someone exercises an option, the OCC verifies the person has the right to exercise it. It then randomly assigns an exercise notice to one of the accounts that is currently short the option.

Optionspeak - My term for the language of options.

Out-of-the-money - A call option with a strike price higher than the price of the underlying, or a put option with a strike price lower than that of the underlying asset. An option with no intrinsic value.

Premium - The price of an option.

Put - An option contract that gives its owner the right to sell the underlying asset at the strike price for a specified time.

Rights - Attributes given to the owner of an option.

Rolling a Position - The process of buying a previously sold option, and selling a different option with a more distant expiration.

Short - The position resulting from selling an asset that is not owned.

Spread - Two simultaneous trades in which you buy one option and sell another.

Standard Deviation - A statistic that describes how closely the data is distributed around the average of the data.

Strike Price - The price at which an option owner can buy or sell the underlying asset.

Time Spread - Two simultaneous trades in which one option is bought and another sold - both with the same strike price in different months.

Time Value - The part of the option premium derived from the volatility and the time remaining until expiration. It is the part of the option premium that is NOT the intrinsic value.

Uncovered Call - A call option sold without owning the underlying. Also called a naked call.

Underlying - The asset from which the option derives its value. It is what the call owner may buy, or the put owner may sell.

Volatility - A measure of the price movement of a stock. It is a measure of the tendency of a stock to make a significant move in a short period of time.

Write - Sell a call when owning the underlying stock.

Appendix B
Calculations

Introduction

Compounding of earnings is an important tool in a wealth-building program. Table B.1 demonstrates the power of compounding. For various time periods, the table shows the amount that $1.00 becomes if it earns 10, 20, or 25%, compounded annually.

The 10% rate was chosen because that is the approximate rate the stock market has returned over many years. The additional returns of 10% and 15% were chosen as illustrative of the extra money you might make using the methods described in this book.

Table B.1
Value of $1 Earning Specified Rates of Return
Compounded Annually

Rate/Years	1	5	10	15	20	25	30
10%	1.10	1.61	2.59	4.18	6.73	10.84	17.45
20%	1.20	2.49	6.19	15.41	38.34	95.40	237.38
25%	1.25	3.05	9.31	28.42	86.74	264.70	807.79

It does not take long for the effects to be substantial. After only ten years, $10,000 growing at 10% compounded annually becomes $25,900. However, it becomes $61,900 if the growth is 20% and $93,100 if the rate of growth is 25%.

Chapter 9

A) **Standard deviation move**. The expected <u>daily</u> movement (M) in the price of a stock priced at S, that has a volatility of V (a percentage, expressed as a decimal), over a period of time (T; there are 252 trading days in a year) is given by the following formula:

M = S x V / SQRT (T)

For a $100 stock that trades with a volatility of 40, the standard deviation move for one day is:

M = 100 x .40 ÷ SQRT (252)

M = 2.5197

This number, M, or 2.52, is the expected standard deviation move. That means the stock will move up or down by no more than this amount, approximately 2 days out of every 3.

B) Premium = Intrinsic Value + Time Value

Intrinsic value is defined as the portion of the premium derived from the fact the option is in-the-money.

How do we determine <u>intrinsic value</u>?

Stock price - (Call) Strike price = **Intrinsic Value**

If the stock price is not greater than the strike price, then the call option has no intrinsic value. The intrinsic value is never less than zero.

How do we determine <u>time value</u>?

Time value = Total Premium - Intrinsic Value

The value of an at-the-money or out-of-the-money option is the time value (because the intrinsic value is zero).

C) "Since your maximum potential profit is based on the amount of time value in the option..."

<u>This is true for an option with an intrinsic value because</u>:

If you are assigned on a call option, you sell your stock for the strike price. When you sold the option you collected

- Intrinsic value

- Time value

The intrinsic value is a rebate of part of your investment in the stock. When you sell your stock at the strike price, you do not gain any additional profit from that intrinsic value.

The time value of the option was reduced to zero when you were assigned. In other words, you collected all the time value, and that is your profit for the transaction.

Here is an example using numbers:

- You are long a stock at 42; your investment is $4200

- You sell an option with a strike price of 40, receiving $650.

  o The intrinsic value of the call is $200

  o The time value is $450 (see above, if this is not clear to you.)

The cost of your investment is reduced by $650 per 100 shares, and is now $3550. The part of the premium that is the intrinsic value is really a refund of part of your cost of the stock. The time value is the additional amount you hope to earn during the life of the option.

If assigned on the option, you earn the full amount of the time value, and you must sell the stock for $4000. Your profit is $450 (4000 - 3550). This profit equals the time value of the option.

Thus, when you sell an option with an intrinsic value, you can consider the intrinsic value as a refund of part of your investment. The remainder of the option premium (the time value) is your profit potential.

D) Table 8.3

The data in this table is calculated as follows:

Take the value of the option from table 8.2. Subtract the intrinsic value, if any, from the premium. The result is the time value of the option.

E) Table 8.4

To calculate the percentage return, you must know how much is invested in the position. Take the stock price of 60 ($6000 for 100 shares) and subtract the amount you received for the call option. As an example, we use the call option with 26 weeks to expiration, a strike price of 50, and a volatility of 60. The price of that option is 1561 (see Table 8.2b). The cost of the position is:

6000 - 1561 = 4439

If you are assigned at expiration, you sell the stock for $5000, so your profit is:

5000 - 4439 = 561

(Note that 561 is the time value of the option.)

The rate of return is 561 ÷ 4439 = 12.64%

These calculations, and those in Table 8.4, have ignored the commissions you pay. Since you have to pay them in the real world, be certain that you calculate your potential return with the cost of commissions included. The total amount you have invested is really the amount calculated in this example, PLUS the commissions that you pay to buy the stock and to sell the call. Those two commissions plus the final commission reduce the net profit. As an example, if you pay a commission of $20 to buy the stock, and another $20 commission to sell the call, then the actual amount of the investment goes from 4439 to 4479. If the commission for selling the stock at expiration is another $20, then the profit is reduced from 561 to 501. The rate of return then becomes:

501 ÷ 4479 = 11.19%

On occasion, you will find the cost of making the trade (commissions) is so high, you will decide the return has become too small to justify making that trade.

Index

Where To Buy This Book

You can buy this book from the author:
http://www.mdwoptions.com/shortbook.html

You can buy this book from the publisher:
http://www.1stbooks.com
Phone: (888)-280-7715

This book may be ordered at any bookstore.

ISBN#: 1-4033-0776-8

About The Author

Mark Wolfinger has been in the options business since 1977. He started as a market maker on the trading floor of the Chicago Board Options Exchange. He also worked for trading companies as an off-floor trader, trainer of newly hired traders, and risk manager. He now serves as an educator of public investors, showing them how they can intelligently and conservatively use stock options.

Born in Brooklyn, New York in 1942, he currently resides in Evanston, Illinois with his life partner Penny and their two cats. He received a BS degree from Brooklyn College and a PhD from Northwestern University.

His website is http://www.mdwoptions.com